INFRASTRU

AS CODᴇ

A Comprehensive Guide to
Managing Infrastructure as Code

Austin Young

TABLE OF CONTENTS

Introduction

In the past few years, there have been a major evolution in IT, and one of such trends has to do with an increased automation and a subsequent decrease in the requirement for manual or human intervention. Automation is a technique that has become an integral part of the economy, and our day-to-day lives. It is reasonable that as the technology we use become even more sophisticated, it should be utilized to automate repetitive tasks and improve efficiency.

Another of such concept or trend is virtualization. Virtualization allows users to create virtual versions of a network resource, a storage device, a server, or an operating system through resources that are usually bound to hardware. It enables you to utilize the full capacity of a physical machine by distributing its capacity among many environments or users. With virtualization, it is possible to build a virtual server location for developers to work outside of the production environment, and hypervisors like Hyper-V and VMWare make it possible to set this up in less than 20 minutes. Obviously, provisioning a virtual workstation is not always so easy. The process could take a lot longer, or require only authorized personnel to perform such actions. A developer might request a virtual workspace for software development and then have to wait for a while for the request fulfillment. This situation raises a need for Infrastructure-as-Code (IaC). IaC represents the point where virtualization and automation meet.

This book attempts to explore all you need to know regarding Infrastructure-as-Code. It will assist you in making informed decisions, if you have plans to implement IaC.

Chapter 1

Infrastructure-as-Code

Infrastructure-as-Code refers to the management and automated provisioning of infrastructure (connection topology, load balancers, virtual machines, servers, and networks) through code rather than using a manual process for configuring systems or devices. It is a practical approach to manage your operational framework, requiring you to build your infrastructure just the same way you build your enterprise applications — using code. It is also known as software-defined or programmable infrastructure. IaC involves using verified and established software development practices utilized in application development. For instance: design patterns, continuous delivery, release promotion, release tagging, automated testing, peer review, version control etc.

IaC is an essential DevOps practice and is utilized together with continuous delivery.

By making use of code to automate the procedure for building and configuring a container or virtual machine, you have a repeatable and fast method for recreating the process. Therefore, if you set up a virtual environment for application development, once you are prepared to deploy, you can replicate the process of building that Virtual Machine (VM) by simply running the same code. There is not much difference between scripting and IaC when it comes to an IT process automation. The issue with scripting is that scripts are normally used to automate fixed steps and are not flexible for complex operations. IaC offers you the flexibility of code within a script-like environment. It dictates what form of infrastructure is produced. Thus, rather than manually configuring a data center, IaC code performs this for you, and becomes your documentation. For example, IaC capabilities built into Ansible – an IT configuration and management tool – can install MySQL database server, verify that it is functioning correctly, create a user password and account, establish a new database, and take out unwanted databases.

Before Infrastructure-as-Code

Within the software development context, a fundamental limitation is the requirement for the environment where newly developed software code is verified to exactly mirror the production environment where the developer deploys the code. This is the only method to ensure that the newly developed code will not clash with existing code definitions – producing conflicts or errors that may compromise the whole system.

Previously, the delivery of software would follow the order below:

- A System Administrator would build a physical server and set up the operating system with every necessary tuning and service packs, to reflect the status of the central operating live system that maintains the production environment.
- Thereafter, a Database Administrator would carry out the same procedure on the support database, and then the machine would be delivered to the testing team.
- The developer would provide the program or code by deploying it to the test environment, and the testing team would run several compliance and operational tests.
- After the newly developed code had gone through the whole process, it would

finally be deployed to the production environment. In many cases, the newly developed code would not operate properly, necessitating additional rework and troubleshooting.

The challenges with manual infrastructure provisioning include:

- High cost: manual provisioning consumes a large amount of human capital. It requires a string of engineers—storage engineers, network engineers, and so on—since it is an extensive process. The higher the number of people required, the higher the costs.
- Reduced agility: manual provisioning relies on a multitude of processes and services. Hence, it is susceptible to lack of adequate agility. This translates to the inability to provide services at your

customers' anticipated speed. It can adversely affect your relationship with them.

- Hardware issues: obtaining the required hardware can consume a lot of time. Waiting for the hardware manufacturer's delivery and production schedules, could take weeks and possibly longer if you require customized hardware. Moreover, one or more components could malfunction or go missing. Additionally, you risk surrendering to the uncertainty of the "human factor" included in the process. This might lead to deviations from expected standards, relative unreliability and inconsistency.

Misconceptions about Infrastructure-as-Code

One common misconception is that Infrastructure-as-Code is sometimes confused with Infrastructure Automation. Infrastructure Automation is the initial step; it is the series of activities that automates repetitive steps, for better management of your infrastructure.

Most companies begin here. Typically, with the understanding that Infrastructure can be managed, maintained, and provisioned better through the automation of monotonous administrative tasks. Examples of Infrastructure Automation may include the utilization of automation to perform:

- Cluster / load-balancer / network / firewall configuration.

- Installation / configuration of application servers, software packages etc.
- Provisioning of cloud instances or servers.

However, Infrastructure Automation by itself does not accomplish the following objectives:

- Tested infrastructure: infrastructure should have been tested in isolation before deploying to production environments.
- Testable infrastructure: all features of infrastructure code should be testable in regard to measurable outcomes.
- Self-healing environments: these refers to infrastructure that can auto-correct and reconcile any departures from its preferred state.
- Disposable infrastructure: destroy and rebuild your whole application

infrastructure, with full confidence it reverts to the same state.

Benefits of Infrastructure-as-Code

IaC provides a lot of advantages to IT teams, these include:

- **Build competitive advantage**
  IaC increases the frequency and speed of releases enabling you to innovate and develop your product quicker. The faster you can deploy new features and resolve issues, the faster you can respond to your customers' requests and build competitive advantage.

- **Adhere to compliance**
  IaC enable you to operate faster while retaining control and adhering to compliance. It can be implemented without surrendering security by utilizing configuration management

techniques, fine-grained controls, and automated compliance policies.

- **Handle complex projects easily**
  IaC allows developers to operate and control the development and infrastructure processes at scale. Due to the consistency and automation facilitated by IaC, developers can handle complex and changing systems competently.

- **Scalable and immutable infrastructure**
  IaC provides the ability for extra resources to be set up during burst periods, enabling horizontal scaling and the capability to replace resources when failure occurs.

- **Use of software delivery principles**
  Capability to promote and apply software delivery principles like code

reviews, peer programming, and version control to Infrastructure leads to fewer unexpected outages and improved change history tracking.

- **Safer change management**
The assurance from standardization allows safer changes to occur, with lower deviation rates.

- **Standardization**
When the establishment of new infrastructure is done through code, there is the guarantee of standardization and a dependable set of instructions. Manual configurations are susceptible to errors and minor alterations, which can create small differences that over time presents substantial nonconformities with the standard.

- **Reduction of capital expenditure (CAPEX)**

  Since IaC enables a developer to complete the tasks of multiple team members, especially from a DevOps perspective, it will result in a significantly improved project CAPEX.

- **Reduction in operating expense (OPEX)**

  If an organization can configure and provision a completely tested and compliant new infrastructural asset in minutes with either limited or even no human interference, it will lead to savings in time and effort, and also mitigate security-related financial risk.

- **Improved customer satisfaction**

  Delivering an excellent service feature within a short period promotes customer satisfaction and improves opinion of IT within a company.

- **Reduced Shadow IT**

  Shadow IT are the infrastructure and applications that are utilized and managed without approval from or knowledge of the company's IT department. A lot of the shadow IT in companies is due to the incapability of IT departments to offer satisfactory and timely response to operational areas regarding IT infrastructure and systems improvements. Shadow IT poses major security risks along with potential unexpected costs for the company. Enabling a quick response to new IT requests through IaC-assisted deployment, do not only ensure greater security and compliance with business technological standards, but is also useful with allocation and budgeting.

- **Better use of time**
  When infrastructure is managed as code, all the repetitive and tedious work is taken over by computers/automation. Hence, reducing the possibility of incomplete work, mistakes, inconsistencies, and other types of human error. It also allows more time for innovation and focus on important, high-value tasks.

- **Version control**
  IaC gets the same benefit that change control provides to application development:
  o Making changes is less daunting since it is easy to revert to a previous version if something goes wrong.

- o New changes can be checked into branches, and tested separately.
- o Code reviews and pull requests increase knowledge sharing, and enhance the overall code quality.
- o Coding standards can be established and maintained.
- o The change history is recorded and available, for better understanding of changes done and why what it was done, over a period of time.
- o The code itself is a form of documentation, to understand how things are built.
- o A distinct source of truth.

- **Redeployment and refinement**
  Since IaC is deployed from code, it is simple to redeploy the very same system somewhere else by simply deploying the code again. Companies can reuse the

same system when they need it. Without having to build from scratch all the time. With accessibility of cloud services on-the-go becoming commonplace, this denotes that a developer can connect to a server remotely and deploy their system from anywhere on earth.

In addition to enabling continuous improvements on the source, IaC also assists us in refining concepts such as monitoring, project structure, and testing. As we practice our process for failures and recovery, we can start to refine our monitoring and testing to cover those characteristics that robust infrastructure should show.

By redeploying over a period of time, we will find new problems that can make our system to operate incorrectly and take the chance to improve every time. As we identify problems, we can set up testing for them in our automated tests suite. Such tests will also serve as regression tests. After a while, our test suite becomes progressively more comprehensive and our assurance in our recovery processes rises.

Challenges of Infrastructure-as-Code

Despite its benefits, IaC poses potential disadvantages. These includes:

- **Accidental destruction**

  Some of the IaC tools are capable of automatically destroying resources if that action is defined in the code. In an automation pipeline, this can sometimes have unintended outcomes.

- **Configuration drift**

  Configuration Drift is the occurrence where running servers within an infrastructure turn out to be more and more different after a while, because of manual ad-hoc updates and changes, and general entropy. Once a machine is built through an IaC workflow, there should not be any interference outside of an automated, coordinated, and compliant maintenance workflow. External or manual updates may cause configuration drifting which may have the potential to produce huge non-compliance or even service downtime.

- **Error replication**
  Since humans write the initial code, there is the possibility of it containing small errors that will only have an impact after a while. The issue here is that for the meantime, there may have been several machines automatically built where such errors exist. Thus,

necessitating the requirement for applying a strong auditing process to the code development.

- **Expertise**

  Expertise is needed to handle most existing IaC tools, and reaching such level involves significant time in training and learning. Some companies would most likely begin by outsourcing services until the employees have undergone training, tools become more user-friendly, or new experts are introduced to the team.

- **Lack of proper planning**

  Once an organization decides to adopt the IaC process, there is the essential need to establish an infrastructure that will facilitate the operation, configuration, and implementation of IaC tools.

How Infrastructure-as-Code Works

In the past so much time, effort, and resources were required all through the software deployment cycle. Involving personnel like operation testers, database administrators, system administrators, and developers. However, with IaC it is possible for the developer to complete all tasks. The common steps followed are:

- The developer writes the code for the application and also set up configuration management related directives that will initiate actions from the virtualization framework, and other environments like the delivery tools, testing tools, database, and more.

- Once the new code is delivered, the configuration management related directives will automatically generate a new virtual test framework containing an application server along with a database instance that precisely mirror the structure of the production environment, both in terms of versioning and service packs as well as production data that is copied to such virtual test framework. This is the Infrastructure-as-Code segment of the process.

- Afterwards, a group of tools will perform essential compliance tests in addition to error discovery and resolution. The newly developed code is then ready to be deployed to the production environment.

Concepts to Know

To properly adopt IaC, you need to understand certain concepts. These include cloud computing, agile development processes and DevOps.

- **Cloud computing**

  This is the provisioning of computing services—including analytics, software, networking, databases, storage, and servers—through the Internet to offer economies of scale, flexible resources, and faster innovation. Usually, you only pay for the cloud services you make use of; helping you scale as your business requirements change, run your infrastructure more proficiently, and lower your operating costs. All clouds are not the same and not one form of cloud computing is appropriate for everyone. Various different service, types, and models have evolved to help provide the correct solutions for your needs. The different methods to deploy cloud services include on hybrid cloud, public cloud or private cloud. The types of cloud services are: Infrastructure-as-a-Service (IaaS), Software-as-a-Service (SaaS), and Platform-as-a-Service (PaaS).

- **Agile software development**
  This is a set of practices and methods focused on the concept of iterative development, where solutions and requirements evolve through cooperation between self-organizing cross-functional teams. Agile is all about delivering business value to clients early, getting feedback, failing fast, iterative and incremental delivery, short cycles, and about people, interaction and collaboration.
  Scrum is a very popular agile framework. It centers on a delivery rate known as a "sprint" and a meeting arrangement that include daily standup meetings, commitment, and planning.

Other agile frameworks include Kanban, Feature Driven Development (FDD), Crystal, Extreme Programming (XP), Lean Software Development, and Dynamic Systems Development Method.

- **DevOps**

  DevOps refers to the combination of tools, practices, and cultural philosophies that increases a company's ability to deliver services and applications at high velocity: improving and evolving products at a quicker pace than organizations utilizing traditional infrastructure management and software development processes. This speed enables companies to better serve their clients and compete more efficiently in the market. DevOps promotes a culture of collaboration, automation, continuous monitoring, continuous delivery, continuous testing and continuous integration.

Goals of Infrastructure-as-Code

The types of results that many organizations and teams look to accomplish through infrastructure-as-code include:

- Solutions to problems are verified by executing, testing, and measuring them, instead of by discussing them in documents and meetings.
- Continuous improvements, instead of carrying out improvements through risky and expensive "big bang" projects.
- Teams are able to recover from failures easily and quickly, rather than assuming that they can completely prevent failure.
- Users are able to specify, set up, and administer the resources they require, without having IT staff to perform this for them.

- IT staff expends their time on valuable tasks that engage their capabilities, rather than on routine, repetitive tasks.
- System changes are routine, without stress or drama for IT staff or users.
- IT infrastructure supports and facilitates change, instead of being a constraint or an obstacle.

Infrastructure-as-Code Principles

The core principles to take note of when planning to adopt IaC include:

- **Dynamic design**

  Prior to Infrastructure-as-Code, it was costly and difficult to update an existing system. Organizations had to make sure that the initial designs are comprehensive, taking several situations and requirements into consideration. This strategy naturally created very complex systems, since it is impossible to correctly estimate the way a system will be utilized in practice. Thus, due to the complexity of the system, it makes it harder for it to be improved and changed, which makes it less efficient in the long run.

The introduction of dynamic infrastructure provisioned from the cloud makes it cost effective and simple to change or update an existing system. Infrastructure and software must be simply designed in order to satisfy existing requirements. Change management should be able to deliver changes quickly and safely. An essential method to make sure that a system can be updated quickly and safely is to frequently make changes. This compels all teams involved to learn good practices for implementing suitable tooling, developing streamlined, efficient processes, and managing processes.

- **Easily reproduced systems**
  IaC would enable you to consistently and smoothly rebuild any component of an infrastructure. Decisions concerning which application and versions to deploy on a server, selecting a hostname, and so forth should be recorded in the tooling and scripts that provision it. The capacity to smoothly build and rebuild any feature of the infrastructure is impressive. It eliminates much of the fear and risk involved when making updates. Failures can be dealt with quickly and with assurance. New environments and services can be provisioned with minimal effort.

- **Idempotence**

  Idempotence has to do with the characteristic that a deployment command would consistently set the selected environment into an equivalent configuration, irrespective of the environment's initial state. Idempotence is achieved through either automatically configuring a current target or by removing the existing target and rebuilding a fresh environment.

  An idempotent process can be repeated a random amount of times and the outcome will be the same as if it had been executed only once. In mathematics, it is idempotent to add zero to a number. This means that your Infrastructure-as-Code can be executed several times and always produce same results, without errors on current resources. The more idempotent your code is, the more it can manage any condition, and always perform the correct action. Idempotence is a critical feature to successfully using IaC.

With IaC, teams make updates to the configuration model version and environment description, which is typically in properly documented code formats like JSON. The release pipeline implements the model to configure selected environments. If the team wants to make updates, they change the source, and not the target. IaC allows DevOps teams to test software in production-like environments from the beginning of the software development cycle. These teams want to provision several test environments on demand and reliably. IaC can also be tested and validated to prevent common deployment problems. Concurrently, the cloud dynamically tears down and provisions frameworks based on IaC definitions.

- **Repeatable processes**

  All actions carried out on your infrastructure must be repeatable. This is made possible by the use of configuration management tools and scripts instead of making changes manually. Efficient infrastructure teams have a resilient scripting culture. If it is possible to automate a task, do that. If it is not possible to automate a task, examine closely and determine if there is a tool or technique that can be utilized, or whether the issue the task is tackling can be managed in a different way.

- **Consistent systems**

  Allowing inconsistencies get into your infrastructure, will make you unable to trust your automation. Assuming there are two infrastructure components that provide the same service – for instance, two database servers within a cluster – the servers must be very similar. Their configuration and system software have to be similar, apart from some unique aspects of configuration, such as their IP addresses.

- **Disposable systems**

  An advantage of dynamic infrastructure is that components can be easily moved, resized, replaced, destroyed, and created. In order to capitalize on this, systems must be designed with the assumption that the infrastructure will constantly change. Software should run continuously even when servers are resized, appear or disappear. The capability to handle changes effectively makes it easier to improve and apply fixes to running infrastructure. This becomes especially significant when sharing extensive cloud infrastructure, where the dependability of the underlying hardware cannot be guaranteed.

Chapter 2

Infrastructure-as-Code Maturity Model

The maturity model for IaC defines five phases of increasing maturity, beginning with a score of -1 and ends at 3, from Regressive phase to Optimizing phase:

Phase -1: Regressive. Here, the processes are reactive, poorly managed, and unrepeatable.

- The documentation for infrastructure procedures, processes, and code are inconsistent, and unavailable to all required parties.
- Infrastructure code is not developed, unit-tested, deployed and managed, as component of a pipeline.
- Infrastructure code is not developed by utilizing industry-standard patterns and tooling.

- Infrastructure provisioning still requires several manual processes.
- Small number of infrastructures are deployed and managed as code.

Phase 0: Repeatable. Here, the processes are documented and partially automated.

- Immutable processes and infrastructure.
- All procedures, processes, and code are available and documented.
- Self-service Command Line Interface (CLI) or Application Programming Interface (API), where internal clients provision their resources.
- Automated security assessment of components and dependencies.
- Utilizes programmatic interfaces for physical devices.
- Infrastructure is deployable as separate components.

- Testing, provisioning, and administration of infrastructure are handled as components of an automated pipeline.
- All infrastructure configuration and code are stored in a streamlined version control system.

Phase 1: Consistent. Here, automated processes are applied across the entire application lifecycle.

- Auto-scaling based on load characteristics defined by the user.
- Secrets are securely managed.
- Template-based configuration files.
- Uses configuration registries.
- Continuously available infrastructure made possible by zero-downtime provisioning.
- Continuous testing for every code checked into the version control system.

- Unit-tests satisfies code-coverage requirements.
- Minimal use of infrastructure tooling that are unsupported or 'home-grown'.
- Fully automated infrastructure provisioning and management.

Phase 2: Quantitatively Managed. Here, the processes are measured and controlled.

- Infrastructure code uses declarative as opposed to imperative programming model.
- All procedures, processes, and code are properly documented in a KMS (Knowledge Management System).
- Infrastructure logging is aggregated and auditable.
- Fully monitored infrastructure with customizable alerting.
- Externalized configuration, without any black box API to alter configuration.

- High availability and fault tolerance of infrastructure and supporting systems.
- Capable of automated rollbacks.
- Makes use of infrastructure definition files.

Phase 3: Optimizing. Here, the focus is on improving processes.

- Cloud-agnostic code that reduces cloud vendor lock-in.
- Adheres to 12-Factor and Cloud Native patterns.
- Increased infrastructure usage and workload density.
- Performance evaluated and monitored against business Key Performance Indicators (KPI).
- Self-optimizing, self-healing, and self-configurable infrastructure.

Chapter 3

Tools for Managing Infrastructure-as-Code

There are fundamentally two categories of tools:

- **Configuration management tools** are utilized to manage, update, and install the software on the infrastructure modules. Examples include Ansible, Chef, Puppet, and SaltStack.

- **Orchestration tools** are utilized to manage, organize, and provision infrastructure components. Examples include Azure Resource Manager, AWS CloudFormation, and Terraform.

Configuration management tools typically default to the mutable infrastructure paradigm. For instance, if you use Ansible to install a new version of Nginx, the software update will be run on current servers, and the updates will happen in-place. On the other hand, orchestration tools regard infrastructure modules as immutable objects. Configuration management tools perform some level of orchestration, and configuration orchestration tools perform some level of configuration administration. Companies can and several times use both categories of tools together. These tools are explained further in the subsequent paragraphs.

- **Ansible**

  This is an infrastructure automation tool developed by Red Hat. Ansible models an infrastructure by describing how the system and components relate to one another, versus managing systems independently. Ansible does not utilize agents, and has its code written in YAML (a data-serialization language) by way of Ansible Playbooks, thus configurations are very simple to comprehend and deploy. Ansible's functionality can also be extended by writing customized Ansible plugins and modules.

- **Chef**

  Companies use this well-known configuration management tool in their continuous delivery and integration processes. With Chef, you are able to create "cookbooks" and "recipes" by utilizing its Ruby-based domain-specific language (DSL). These cookbooks and recipes specify the exact steps required to achieve the preferred configuration of your utilities and applications on current servers. This is referred to as a "procedural" perspective to configuration management, since you describe the procedure needed to reach your desired state. This tool is cloud-agnostic and functions with many cloud service vendors such as OpenStack, Google Cloud Platform, Microsoft Azure, AWS, and more.

- **Puppet**

  Puppet is another well-known configuration management tool that assists engineers to deliver software continuously. Making use of Puppet's Ruby-based DSL, a company can define the preferred end-state of their infrastructure as well as the specifications. Then Puppet automatically applies the desired state and resolve any incorrect changes. This is referred to as the "declarative" approach, since you declare what your configuration should look like, after which, Puppet determines how to get there. This is the main difference between Chef and Puppet. In addition,

Puppet is mainly targeted for system administrators, while Chef mainly targets developers. Puppet works well with leading cloud providers like VMware, Google Cloud, Azure, and AWS, allowing you to automate through multiple clouds.

- **SaltStack**
  This differentiates itself from other configuration management tools like Puppet and Chef by taking an "Infrastructure-as-Data" approach, rather than "Infrastructure-as-Code." What this signifies is that even though SaltStack's declarative configuration patterns, are written in Python, they are language-agnostic (that is, there is no need to learn a particular DSL to develop them) and hence are more easily understood and read. One other

difference is that SaltStack facilitates remote execution of commands, while Puppet and Chef's configuration code have to be gotten from their servers.

- **Google Cloud Deployment Manager** and **Azure Resource Manager**

  If you are utilizing Google Cloud Platform or Microsoft Azure, these cloud service providers provide their own IaC tools.

  Azure Resource Manager enables you to control access to resources via user permissions, arrange dependent resources into clusters that can be deleted or deployed in a single action, outline the infrastructure and dependencies of an application in templates, and so on.

Google Cloud Deployment Manager
provides many similar services to
automate a GCP infrastructure module.
You can view deployments through a
console user interface, preview the
changes that will be done before
deploying, build templates using Python
or YAML, and so on.

- **AWS CloudFormation**

  This configuration orchestration tool
  allows the coding of an infrastructure, in
  order to automate deployments.
  CloudFormation can only be used with
  and is deeply integrated into AWS, and
  the templates in CloudFormation can be
  built with YAML along with JSON.
  CloudFormation allows previewing of
  proposed changes to an AWS
  infrastructure stack, for you to
  understand how they might affect your

resources. It also controls dependencies between these resources. CloudFormation utilizes Rollback Triggers to return infrastructure stacks to a former deployed state if issues are detected. This guarantees that updates and deployment of infrastructure is performed in a controlled manner. Infrastructure stacks can be deployed across multiple AWS regions and accounts with one CloudFormation template.

- **Terraform**
  HashiCorp develops this infrastructure-provisioning tool. It automates changes with very little human interaction, builds a graph of specified resources, creates "execution plans" that describe exactly what will occur when the code is run, and allows you to represent your

infrastructure as code. Terraform utilizes its own DSL known as HashiCorp Configuration Language (HCL), which is JSON-compatible and is utilized to create the configuration files that illustrate the infrastructure modules to be installed. Terraform is cloud-agnostic. It enables the automation of infrastructure stacks from several cloud service providers simultaneously in addition to integrating other third-party services. Terraform plugins can be written to add new improved functionality to the platform.

- **Vagrant**
  This is another IaC tool developed by HashiCorp. Vagrant focuses on easily and quickly creating development environments that utilize a small

number of virtual machines, rather than large cloud infrastructure environments spanning numerous servers across multiple cloud vendors. Vagrant runs on virtual machine solutions from AWS, VMWare, VirtualBox, and any other cloud vendor, and also functions well with tools like Puppet and Chef.

- **Docker**

  Docker assists in easily creating containers that package dependencies and code together so applications can function in any environment, from a local workstation to the servers of any cloud service provider. YAML is used to build configuration files known as Dockerfiles. These are the blueprints to create the container images that has everything (settings, system tools and libraries, runtime, and code) needed to run a software. Since it increases an application's portability, Docker has been particularly valuable in organizations that utilize multi-cloud or hybrid environments. The usage of Docker containers has risen exponentially over the last few years and many view it as the future of virtualization.

Chapter 4

Infrastructure-as-Code Approaches

There are two major approaches to IaC – imperative and declarative. In both approaches, the configurations for IaC is done on a template, wherein the user describes the resources needed for every server in the infrastructure. This template is used to verify that a system is accurately configured, and if it is not, then put it in the correct setup. Templates can be built as a collection containing layers of resources, like in AWS CloudFormation, which creates a stack. The imperative and declarative approaches are explained further in subsequent paragraphs.

- **Imperative approach**

  This defines commands that allow the infrastructure to get to the preferred state. Imperative IaC systems describe the "how" in terms of systems configuration. For most companies, the earliest form of IaC involved the use of basic installation scripts. In the initial step, an administrator creates a script to automatically install a part of a software on a server, rather than logging into the server and performing that action directly. Over time, engineers merged these scripts to build a complete system configuration script. Thus, simplifying manual systems administration. This simplification leads to more consistent and predictable builds.

Imperative IaC has the advantage of being very easy to set up and simpler for management to comprehend. However, due to this simplicity, Imperative IaC often requires more manual work from system administrators to keep all scripts up-to-date. Updates to installed applications can break current scripts, thus administrators are stuck fixing the issues.

Object-oriented languages can be utilized for imperative programming (example: Java and C++). A tool like Chef can be utilized in the declarative way, but also imperatively as required. With Chef, users outline commands and their order of execution in configuration instructions known as Recipes, which can also be arranged into Cookbooks for simpler management. Chef Recipes are organized as consecutive lists of commands.

- **Declarative approach**
This outlines the intended, desired state of the infrastructure; however, it does not explicitly outline the steps to get to

that state. Declarative IaC systems describe the "what" in terms of systems configuration. When using a declarative approach, administrators do not describe the steps to build a server. Instead, they supply a list of requirements, after which a third-party software does the task of installing the necessary application. These requirements can be simple (for example, list of software packages) or complicated (for example, complete web of codependent servers).

Declarative IaC installations does not require a lot of manual modification of scripts since external software controls the installation process. Tools like Puppet or Chef manage the process of reconciling system dependencies. Administrators do not typically face as many issues with software upgrades, because the software takes care of software interdependency for them.

An example of a well-down declarative programming language is SQL. The templates in AWS CloudFormation are created in the declarative form of Infrastructure-as-Code. Puppet is declarative: the system administrator defines a desired end-state and the tool tries to reach it. Its DSL is utilized for creating high-level specifications of desired server state, instead of actions and instructions to be executed. Manifests are Puppet files that holds configuration information and can be utilized any amount of times to realize similar results. If the preferred end-state has already been achieved, Puppet simply ignores the component in question. Users only have to worry about the preferred end-state of the system that will be configured, not the series of steps required to reach there.

Chapter 5

Mutable Infrastructure

Mutable infrastructure refers to IT server infrastructure that can be updated and modified in-place frequently. Traditionally, server infrastructures have been mutable because of the greater short-term versatility that the mutable approach offers. However, mutable infrastructure occurs at the cost of consistency and predictability between various server deployments. Administrators and engineers working with this form of infrastructure can deploy new code directly on top of existing servers, tweak configuration documents on a server-by-server basis, downgrade or upgrade packages manually and SSH into their servers. Simply put, these servers are mutable, and can be modified after they are created. Infrastructure containing mutable servers are sometimes known as artisanal, traditional, or mutable.

Challenges with Mutable Infrastructure

There are several reasons mutable infrastructure made up of traditional, long-lived features is not fully capable of running modern, distributed solutions in the cloud.

- More failures and slower deployments. When infrastructure is composed of snowflake components brought about by mutable maintenance methods (whether through configuration management tools or scripts), there is so much more that can fail. Departing from a straight-from-source-control process denotes that truly knowing the state of an infrastructure is impossible. Dependability is lost as infrastructure operates in irregular ways and time is lost debugging the runtime and chasing down configuration drift.

- Increased operational complexity. The growth of distributed service frameworks and the utilization of dynamic scaling leads to vastly more things to keep track of. Utilizing mutable maintenance methods for patching configurations or updates across a huge number of compute instances is a time wasting, error-prone, and difficult process.

- Identifying errors and threats to mitigate harm. Longstanding, mutable systems depend on identifying threat or error to prevent damage.

- Provisioning servers is typically a long process owing to the requirement for manual configuration.

- Changes to the server might not be documented, making it difficult to track versions.
- Technical issues are hard to reproduce or identify because every server has a distinct configuration, a phenomenon sometimes known as "configuration drift."

Immutable Infrastructure

This takes Infrastructure-as-Code to the next level. Immutable infrastructure is a model for infrastructure maintenance and deployment, wherein servers are never altered after they are deployed. To fix the software or make any update, new servers are built from the base image with the changes included. After validations, they are deployed and the previous servers are decommissioned. To easily rollback and distribute, you can tag and version control your images. The image has all the configuration, runtime dependencies and application code – in essence, the state required for the software to operate as expected.

This approach to managing servers came as a response to traditional methods (mutable infrastructure) that depend on one-off changes or configuration management tools to patch, update, and maintain running server instances. Increasingly, this method alone can cause a server's state to slowly drift from its initial definition, which can become time consuming and difficult to debug and manage (creating what is referred to as a snowflake server. Snowflake servers are servers that are manually managed, updated frequently and tweaked in-place, leading to a distinct environment). Enabling configuration synchronization can assist in keeping servers up-to-date, but any component that the configuration management tool is not managing can potentially introduce an area of drift. As a concept, an immutable server naturally developed due to the Phoenix Server pattern. The Phoenix Server pattern asserts that servers must be frequently destroyed and then recreated using a base image. Immutability takes it a step further and limits a production server to make sure it is never changed.

This concept is comparable to occurrences in other industries such as consumer electronics. It has become typical for cell phones to have storage that cannot be replaced, and batteries that cannot be changed. Therefore, those devices are immutable and the entire device will have to be replaced if an upgrade is required. This offers a level of uniformity that makes it easier to support. Irrespective of the number of mobile devices in service, there is accurate knowledge of the exact specifications of each device and can simply replace as-is in case of an issue.

Infrastructure-as-Code is the ideal approach to create immutable infrastructure. Running it on public cloud providers and virtualized platforms, leads to what is commonly known as DevOps.

Difference between Immutable and Mutable Infrastructure

The main difference between them is that mutable infrastructure is continuously tuned, patched and updated to meet the ongoing requirements of the objective it serves, while the state of an immutable infrastructure does not get deviated or changed once constructed.

The two forms of infrastructure management vary greatly in their method to how servers must be handled. In traditional mutable infrastructures, the servers were irreplaceable, distinct systems that should be kept running all the time. The servers are managed manually, unique, and one of a kind. On the other hand, in immutable infrastructures, the servers are expendable and easy to scale with automated tools or replicate. No individual server is unique or indispensable.

Mutable infrastructure is an old infrastructure paradigm that precedes the core technologies, like cloud computing and virtualization that make immutable infrastructures practical and possible. Before cloud computing and virtualization became widely available and possible, server infrastructure was focused on physical servers. These servers were time-consuming and costly to create; the preliminary setup could take a long time due to the length of time it took to make orders for new hardware, configuring the machine, and then installing it. Mutable infrastructure has its foundation here. Since it was costly to

replace a server, it was very practical to keep
making use of the existing servers for as long
as you can with as little service interruption as
possible. This signified that there were so
many in-place changes for regular updates
and deployments, but also for patches, tweaks,
and ad-hoc fixes when something fails. The
consequence of regular manual updates is that
servers can get hard to recreate, making each
one a distinct and fragile feature of the entire
infrastructure. The advent of cloud computing
and virtualization represented a defining
moment in infrastructure management.
Virtual servers were less costly, even at scale,
and these servers could be built and destroyed
in minutes rather than days or weeks. This led
to the possibility of new server management
and deployment workflows techniques for the
first time, such as using cloud APIs or
configuration management to provision new
servers automatically, programmatically and

quickly. The feasibility of the immutability principle is due to the low cost and speed of building new virtual servers.

Traditional mutable infrastructures initially came to be when the utilization of physical servers determined what was achievable in their administration, and continued to advance as technology improved through the years. The paradigm of updating servers after it has been deployed is still common nowadays. Conversely, immutable infrastructures were intended from the start to depend on virtualization-based technologies for quick provisioning of architecture features, like virtual servers in cloud computing.

Benefits of Immutable Infrastructure

There are numerous advantages of immutable infrastructure if applied properly to your application. These include:

- **No configuration drift**

  Every configuration change in an immutable infrastructure is executed by checking a modified image into version control along with the documentation and using a unified, automated deployment process to deploy additional servers with that image. Access to the servers through SSH is sometimes completely limited. This prevents hard-to-reproduce or complicated setups by reducing the risk of configuration drift and snowflake servers. This also prevents occurrences where someone needs to alter a production server that is not well understood, which runs a great risk of error and initiating downtime or unintended behavior.

- **Simple recovery and rollback processes**

  Making use of version control to maintain image history also aids in handling production problems. Since the same procedure that is utilized to deploy new images could also be utilized to rollback to older versions, it creates additional resilience and reduces recovery time when controlling downtime.

- **Easy horizontal scaling and consistent staging environments**

  Since all servers use similar creation process, deployment edge cases does not occur. This prevents inconsistent or messy staging environments by allowing it to be easy to replicate the production environment, as well as simplifies horizontal scaling by consistently allowing you to insert more identical servers to an infrastructure.

- **Fewer deployment failures and known-good server state**
  Every deployment in an immutable infrastructure is implemented by provisioning new servers with the aid of a version-controlled and validated image. Consequently, these deployments do not rely on a server's previous state, and so cannot fail — or only partly complete — due to it. After new servers have been provisioned, they can be validated before being used, reducing the actual deployment procedure to one update, to ensure the availability of the new server (for example, updating a load balancer). This means that deployments become atomic: either the deployments complete successfully or there is no

change. This makes deploying far more dependable and makes sure you know the state of all servers in the infrastructure. In addition, this process makes it simple to implement rolling releases or a blue-green deployment, meaning no downtime.

- Portability, especially when utilizing Docker containers.
- It is easier to test and implement microservices for an extensive application.

Drawbacks of Immutable Infrastructure

The following are the challenges associated with immutable infrastructure:

- The improved dynamism and agility of immutable infrastructure can oftentimes be misaligned with conventional IT security practices.

- The infrastructure is unable to be altered in-place. For example, when a zero-day vulnerability occurs, all servers with similar configuration must get a security update.
- Possible increase in resource cost and usage depending on how many times servers are decommissioned and redeployed in a particular time period.
- Small quick fixes entail a full redeploy.
- Higher initial overhead to implement the infrastructure and learn new tooling.

Make an Object Reproducible

This involves three steps:

- Automate the process.

- Create scripts that will develop and assemble the features into the object as outlined in the documentation.
- Document the processes involved in creating the object. Each version of the scripts and documentation should be tracked via some type of version control tool so modifications can be recorded.

Build an Immutable Server Image

The server image is the basis of an effective immutable infrastructure. Below is an outline of the steps needed to create a source-of-truth production image that could be reliably deployed across several servers:

- Create a base image to boot an instance of a server on your selected cloud-hosting platform. This will include baseline features like the installed packages and running Linux distribution.

- Utilize a configuration management tool, such as Jenkins or Chef, to bring your server to the state required to host your software code.

- Build a new server image using the configured instance of the server.

- Build a new instance on the test server containing the new server image (includes all dependencies, configuration and application code).

- Run predetermined automated tests to assess the new server image.

- Install the new image in production, if the tests pass.

- Destroy the old production server and store the destroyed server image.

Quickly Create Images

The following are possible solutions that you can consider to test and build server images more quickly.

- **Cache installation files**

  To optimize the time required to run installation and updates on the server image, cache the source files nearer to where the image will be created. This could mean moving internal software repositories to a nearer location on the cloud or network, using caching proxies, or mirroring package repositories.

- **Reduce the operating system(OS) image**

  The time required to save server images and boot server instances increases with the scope of the OS installation. Hence, teams can improve the process by reducing the base operating system down to the lowest level—packages and files actually needed for their use case. The benefits of this include reduced surface area of attacks, and reduced time to boot servers enabling automated recovery and scaling. However, one risk with using a minimal image is that there may be an increase in the size and number of packages deployed during the image update. To handle this, use a layered approach. Start with a basic OS distribution, and then add the required files into a base image, that is eventually used to create role-specific images.

- **Work on updates in a sandbox**
  Making use of automation to make changes turns out to be truly painful when you want to run through the continuous delivery pipeline to see if a simple change works. It is vital that

people working on infrastructure code, test and make changes locally before checking them into version control and starting the pipeline. A team making a modification that will result in producing a new server image, can rapidly create the existing server version locally, in order for them to try out changes and validate before committing. To avoid "edit-commit-test-fail-edit-commit" loops, it should be feasible to execute the automated tests locally. An example of a sandbox tool for software development is Vagrant.

- **Build images on chroot**
  Chroot is a command to "change root". Instead of configuring a server instance after booting it, it may be viable to install a boot disk on an existing machine, and make modifications to it

as a fixed directory structure. Running
update and installation packages in a
chroot jail assists in making this
possible. An example is the Packer
amazon-chroot builder used for AWS
AMI images.

- **Layer images**
Using several layers of images is another
way to minimize the time required to
update servers. For instance, a base
server image can contain the operating
system, with every package updated and
installed. New images are created from
this base image, so just the newest
changes have to be implemented. The
base server image may be updated once
in a while, especially when operating
system packages and other similar files
are released. This strategy works
particularly well when there are several

images for different services and
applications, all built on the same
operating system distribution. In some
situations, it makes sense to have
several layers of images. For instance, a
team in a company may have a base
operating system image used to build all
types of servers as well as a Java server
image that includes an application
server and the JDK, which is then
utilized to build server images for
separate applications.

- **Minimize test bloat**
  Over time, automated test suites can
  come to be slow-running and heavy.
  Make certain that tests are running fast
  and pruned, in order for them not to
  overwhelm the change process.

Components needed to Implement Immutable Infrastructure

Technically, it is possible to execute an immutable infrastructure without any software design principles, tooling or automation, by simply observing the essential principle of immutability. Nonetheless, the components below are necessary for practicality at scale:

- **Dedication from operations and engineering teams** to work together and commit to the infrastructure approach. Even though the end-product looks simple, there are various moving parts involved in an immutable infrastructure implementation, and a single person cannot know all of it. Moreover, some aspects of working in this infrastructure can be different or outside of some employees' comfort zones, like doing special tasks without shell access, or debugging.

- **A volatile, stateless application layer** that includes your immutable servers. Whatever is here can get decommissioned and recreated quickly whenever (volatile) without losing any data (stateless).

- **A service-oriented architecture**, separating the infrastructure into logically discrete modules that communicate across a network. This enables you to make the most of cloud computing solutions that are similarly service-oriented (e.g. PaaS, IaaS, and SaaS).

- **Complete automation of the entire deployment pipeline**, preferably including post-creation image verification. Creating this automation adds considerably to the initial cost of implementing immutable infrastructure, but this is a single-time cost that amortizes out quickly.

- **Servers in a cloud-computing framework** or another virtualized environment (such as containers). Here, the key is to have remote instances with quick provisioning from base images, in addition to automated management for destruction and creation through an API or similar.

- **A persistent data layer composed of centralized logging and external data stores.** Centralized logging would contain additional details regarding a server's deployment, for example: Git commit SHA or image identification through a version. Since servers are disposable (and regularly disposed of) in immutable infrastructure, storing metrics and logs externally facilitates debugging even when there is restricted shell access or after a server has been destroyed. Any other ephemeral or stateful data, such as block or object storage (either self-managed or cloud-provided) and Database-as-a-Service/cloud databases are also included here. If the servers are volatile, you cannot depend on local storage, so you need to save that data elsewhere.

Containers and Immutable Infrastructure

Containers are a well-known element for immutable infrastructure since containers make it conceivable to create several instances of a service or an application with the aid of container images. When updates have to be implemented on the service or application, the container image is modified, and then new container instances are created to replace the old instances. Updates can be exhaustively vetted before launching the new instance. It is not required to reconfigure the service or application instances while they are in operation. The team involved would have to decide on how to configure and build the host servers utilized to run the containers. Several teams will create these hosts by adopting the immutable model. The process for adopting the immutable model is easier to manage than the process where applications are executed directly on servers, without the use of containers. Container hosts only need the software used to manage and run container instances. Hence, they tend to change less frequently and can be smaller.

An example of a container is Docker. Docker Containers were created to be immutable. It comes with many built-in utilities to assist in managing container images. If you modify the image definition of a container, then you have developed a new image. The Docker commit command will build a new image, with the original image remaining unchanged. The Docker tag command enables easy tagging of Docker image commit. Other valuable metadata can be inserted to Docker images to assist in identifying image inheritance. Another advantage to utilizing Docker containers to execute an immutable infrastructure is that Docker helps manage stateful components or data persistence, such as the database of an application. Stateful components cannot easily be decommissioned and redeployed by utilizing a server image. The volume feature of a Docker container will exist outside a given container's lifecycle, allowing containers to be destroyed when needed and generate a new one using the persisted data.

Factors to Consider Regarding the Immutability of Containers

Containers are beneficial in deploying applications without worrying that unforeseen configuration issues will create security vulnerabilities or disrupt a running application. However, it is necessary to realize that not all components of a container are immutable. A container image is immutable, but some other important characteristics and parts of the container environment are not. Consistent monitoring of the environment is needed to stay ahead of any potential security, stability and performance issues. The factors to consider include:

- **Change in dependencies**

  Updating container images may lead to application changes that disrupt dependencies. For instance, a container-based microservice that relies on a different container-based microservice to operate may stop working correctly if there is an update on the container image upon which the microservice is built. This is true if the update is executed through immutable container images. That is to say, immutable container images does not avert the risk of application updates that break the multifaceted stack on which your software relies on to function properly.

- **Change in endpoints**

  In most container environments, updates to network endpoints would not cause problems since the changes will be identified automatically through service discovery. Nevertheless, service discovery can fail sometimes. Changes to endpoint configurations can bring about unexpected performance issues if they are not handled properly.

- **Change in host infrastructure configurations**
  Most of the host servers for container frameworks are built using traditional operating systems, whose configuration are always changing. Theoretically, changes to the host ought not to affect applications that are isolated within containers, however, in practice they can. Changes in host infrastructure might interrupt storage services used by containers. For example, some modifications in networking resources could cause problems for containers.

- **Change in orchestration tools**

  One of the benefits of containers is that it is easier to move software from one environment to another. Occasionally, when migrating you need to change not just the host servers, but also the orchestration tools. For instance, ECS container service provided by AWS runs an in-built orchestrator that is not obtainable on other platforms. Transferring a container environment from or to ECS may therefore require a change in orchestrators.

- **Changes in the container environment's scale**

  The number of service and application instances fluctuates due to shifts in requests and new services inserted into the container environment. There can also be a change in data storage requirements. As scale fluctuates, it also affects the functionality of other tools in the environment. For instance, you may not have to worry much concerning load balancing when the environment is small. Yet, when you have tons of containers running, an inadequately configured load balancer can cause severe application performance problems.

Common Tools for Immutable Infrastructure

The simplest tooling may already be offered by your cloud provider's clustering and imaging solution. For instance, Oracle Cloud Infrastructure (OCI) can be utilized to generate images. Consider instance pools and instance configurations if you require a cluster of servers rather than just one. Other cloud solutions have equivalent mechanisms to create images and instance pools. Some common tools include:

- **Packer**

  This unique tool can quickly create a base image, deploy an application and its configurations (with the aid of other Configuration Management and IaC tools) and generate a base image that can be used to spin up servers. Packer provides plugins for the prominent CI/CD tools, so this will be triggered in the pipeline as a step in the build process.

  Step1: Packer Builder reads the specifications from a JSON file, and then spins up a running instance from the common image. This is done on any cloud framework like Google Cloud Platform, Azure, Amazon Web Services or OCI.

Step2: Packer Provisioner configures and deploys the applications, libraries and configurations by making use of a configuration management tool like Salt, Ansible, Puppet or Chef.

Step3: Packer stores the generated image in your account. You can then utilize that image to spin up your cluster or server. Adding the Jenkins build number and the Git commit id to the name of the image can provide traceability from the running server down to the code version it was built from.

- **Spinnaker**

  Spinnaker is a tool initially developed by Netflix and extended by Google. It is an extensive end-to-end build and deploy tool for immutable infrastructure. The reasons why Spinnaker assists with immutable infrastructure are:

- It supports rollout/deployment strategies (like rolling update, canary deployment, red-black deployment), versioning and importantly offers an easy way of rolling back to earlier versions of an infrastructure with two clicks.
- It is an opinionated CI/CD pipeline tool with batteries-included, that generates a machine image (same way as container images). Internally, Spinnaker uses Packer to create images.
- It is deeply integrated with clouds, enabling it to control other resources (such as load balancers) and offers a single glass pane to manage your resources spanning across several cloud providers, accounts, regions and zones.

Chapter 6

Security

Automating the infrastructure deployment process makes compliance and security testing more important, since with IaC, it is simpler and easier to make extremely impactful changes to a cloud framework. This is the downside of agility. In the cloud, where simple configuration modifications can leave private servers and sensitive data exposed to the public, the security consequences of automation are profound.

Below are some phases that companies can go through to ensure adequate security:

- **Manual security assessment**
  This involves manually inspecting the production infrastructure after deployments, and appraising the templates/architecture before deploying it to a production environment. Even

though DevOps teams are proficient in creating Terraform and AWS CloudFormation templates, most teams still practicing traditional security approaches are not aware of these technologies. Examining the security perspective of these templates is a slow, labor-intensive process that requires substantial back and forth between security and operations, putting a brake on CI/CD pipelines.

- **Static (infrastructure) code analysis before deployment**
  Here, we handle templates same as any other software code and perform compliance and security unit-tests after committing the code as part of the established CI process. This brings compliance and security very close to the source, drastically reducing the

operational difficulty of approaches and the time to detection.

- **Testing and deploying in sandbox environments**

  IaC principle of repeatable processes make this possible, where the template is initially deployed into a provisional environment. Automated (and occasionally manual) tests validate that there were no compliance and security regressions before the changes are pushed to a production environment. An automated CI/CD pipeline orchestrates all of that, and then terminates the provisional environment. While this strategy is effective in making sure that code pushed to production environments meets compliance and security requirements, it can be costly in terms of solution, resources and time complexity.

- **Continuous monitoring of production environments**

  Here, the production environment is monitored continuously for compliance and security violations. This is typically achieved using dedicated cloud security solutions that provide continuous compliance and security testing. While being naturally reactive, this form of monitoring covers both automated changes along with manual changes.

Chapter 7

Best Practices for Implementing Infrastructure-as-Code

In order to take full advantage of IaC, you have to incorporate three essential components: automation tools needed to write the code, an established DevOps culture, and Agile development processes. Agile development and DevOps go hand-in-hand as both aim to effectively speed up development processes and empower the software development team to produce quality work. With the basics of IaC covered, it is now time to examine some best practices for its implementation.

- **Exercise caution when presenting IaC tools to beginners**
  IaC makes reconfiguring and deploying server environments very simple, but that comes with some challenges. While

beginners can spin up multiple instances within minutes, they can also cause a huge amount of damage within a short period. Go slow when introducing IaC to the DevOps team members, and make certain that users have guidance and supervision, especially when trying something new.

- **Version control**

  Always maintain records of everything: templates, configuration files, and automation. Version-control systems like Git allows users to collaborate by offering a centralized repository where every template, configuration, code, etc. can be found. Git also lets users restore or review older versions of files. Some of the reasons to version control everything include:

- **Visibility**. Every team member can see when there are new changes checked into the version control system, facilitating situational awareness. Someone may observe that a change is missing an important aspect. If an incident occurs, team members are aware of latest commits that may have caused it.
- **Rollback.** When a change leads to a defect—and especially when several changes break something—it is beneficial to be able to roll back to the previous working state.
- **Actionable.** Version Control Systems (VCS) can automatically initiate actions after a change is committed. Thus, enabling CI/CD delivery pipelines.
- **Traceability**. VCS provides history for changes done, who made them,

and theoretically, context about why
the change was done. This is vital
when debugging problems.

- ○ **Correlation.** When artifacts,
  configurations, scripts, and every
  other related components are in the
  version control system and correlated
  by version numbers or tags, it can be
  beneficial for detecting and resolving
  problems that are more complex.

- **Proper documentation**
  With IaC, the steps to implement a
  process are recorded in the tools,
  definition files, and scripts that actually
  execute the process. Only a limited
  number of additional documentations
  are required to get people started. These
  include diagrammatic representations
  and setup instructions of your
  architecture, as they are useful in getting

employees acquainted to the system and for sharing knowledge.

- **Codify everything**

  All the specifications or definitions for the infrastructure should be clearly written in the configuration files. The configuration files are essential since they describe the exact components that will be used in the IaC setup, along with their relationship to each other. The production IaC code should be deployed rapidly and seamlessly; this cannot occur when users login and find themselves having to make manual adjustments. The infrastructure component could be a network configuration (like a load balancer rule), part of a server (like a user account), a server or many other things. Various tools have different names for this: for instance, manifests (Puppet), recipes (Chef), or playbooks (Ansible).

Any change needed in a configuration, application, or server must be outlined in the code. You can convert configuration files into templates to facilitate greater reusability and flexibility. Settings specific to servers or applications must also be coded, typically in variable files. When building the automation, it is critical to evoke idempotence: No matter how often the code is implemented, the result should always be the same. Same input, same output. For example, when writing a code to modify a file, you have to make sure that if you execute the same code again, the file will be the same. Some examples to codify cloud and traditional infrastructure include:

- **Vagrantfile** – for local development and testing.
- **Capistrano/Fabric** – for remote command implementation and deployment.
- **Dockerfile** – for container management.
- **Chef/Puppet modules** – for network management.
- **Bash scripts/PowerShell, Chef/Puppet modules** – for configuration management.
- **APIs** – for DNS management. Several scripts typically interact with DNS system through APIs.
- **Python scripts, YAML, CloudFormation, Terraform** – for infrastructure (virtual or physical servers) management.

- **Modularity**

  With IaC, it is vital to think about reusability. The code should be scalable and reusable. Microservices architecture is a known trend in the world of software development, where application is built by creating smaller, modular elements of code, which can be deployed separately from the rest of an application's components. IaC can apply the same concept. The infrastructure can be broken down into individual stacks or modules, and then combined in an automated manner. This approach have a few benefits. To start with, there is improved access control. For instance, modularizing the infrastructure code can block access to certain components for some users – especially users who do not have the expertise or are not yet familiar with specific parts of the infrastructure code. In addition, modular infrastructure naturally restricts the amount of modifications that can be done to the configuration. Smaller updates/changes makes it easier to detect bugs and allow the team to become more agile.

Moreover, if the microservices development approach is utilized, a configuration template could be created for each individual microservice to ensure infrastructure uniformity. Then every microservice can be connected via messaging interfaces or HTTP.

Some of the advantages of smaller updates/changes include:

o It is faster to reverse or fix a small change.
o It is motivating to get improvements done and issues resolved. Having

large batches of uncompleted work piling up, with no progress, is demotivating.

o It is less work and easier, to validate a small change and ensure it is solid.

o A little problem can delay many things in a large group of changes from moving forward, even when there are no issues in the other changes within the group.

o It is easier to identify the cause of an issue when it is a small change than when it is a large batch of changes.

Git submodules can be used to execute modular components at scale. With Git submodule functionality, you can have an additional Git repository in your infrastructure's subdirectory, as a code repository. This additional Git repository retains its own history and does not affect the history of the IaC repository. It can be used to add internal and external dependencies, as well as manage access control since you will be maintaining different Git repositories – each with its own write and read permissions. When pulling or cloning an IaC repository, submodules are not automatically checked out. You will have to give explicit command to checkout or update Git submodule.

- **Continuous testing, integration and deployment**
IaC code should be continuously tested in order to identify areas where the code is either not working as expected, or is returning unexpected errors. In addition to testing the dependability of a deployment, it is necessary to create tests that will examine the current IaC

setup to make sure it is secure. Testing should be rigorously implemented on infrastructure configurations to make certain that no post-deployment issues exists. Depending on your requirements, a range of test types – integration, regression, unit and lots more – should be done. Automated tests can be built to run each time there is a change in the configuration code.

Security of the infrastructure should also be continually tested and monitored. DevSecOps is a developing practice where the security team works alongside developers to incorporate security testing and threat detection from the beginning of the development life cycle. By increasing collaboration between development, security and testing teams, you can identify bugs and threats sooner in the development process and thus resolve them before going live.

With a comprehensive continuous integration process, configuration templates can be set up multiple times in several environments such as QA, test, and Dev. Developers can then work within every one of these environments with the same infrastructure configurations. This will diminish the presence of errors that may be damaging to the infrastructure when it is deployed to production.

- **Immutable infrastructure**
  Immutable infrastructure affirms that IT infrastructure features are to be replaced for each deployment, rather than been changed in-place. You can develop code and deploy an

infrastructure module once, use it several times, and never modify it. If you want to modify your configuration, you would need to terminate that module and create a new one. An immutable infrastructure restricts the effect of non-documented changes to the module, avoids configuration drift, and provides consistency. It also increases security and makes it easier to troubleshoot due to the absence of configuration edits.

Chapter 8

Conclusion

Infrastructure-as-Code refers to the management and automated provisioning of infrastructure (connection topology, load balancers, virtual machines, servers, and networks) through code rather than using a manual process for configuring systems or devices. It is an essential DevOps practice and is utilized together with continuous delivery. It offers many advantages such as standardization, scalable and immutable infrastructure, reduced capital and operation expense, improved customer satisfaction and much more. IaC can be approached either imperatively or declaratively.

Immutable infrastructure is a model for infrastructure maintenance and deployment, wherein servers are never altered after they are deployed. To fix the software or make any update, new servers are built from the base image with the changes included. After validations, they are deployed and the previous servers are decommissioned. To quickly create images: cache installation files, reduce the operating system(OS) image, work on updates in a sandbox, build images on chroot, layer images, and minimize test bloat.

Additionally, security is very important when adopting IaC, some of the practices you can implement include: manual security assessment, static (infrastructure) code analysis before deployment, testing and deploying in sandbox environments, continuous monitoring of production environments, modularity, immutable infrastructure, exercise caution when presenting IaC tools to beginners, continuous testing, integration and deployment, codify everything, proper documentation, and version control.

Other Books by Same Author

- Productive DevOps: Your Complete Handbook on Building a Dependable, Agile and Secure Organization
- Cloud Computing: A Comprehensive Guide to Cloud Computing

Printed in Great Britain
by Amazon